A Beginner's Guide to

INTARSIA KNITTING

11 simple inspiring projects with easy to follow steps

by Quail Studio

contents

introduction

A Beginner's Guide to Intarsia Knitting is straight from our design team at Quail Studio and offers the perfect introduction to working with colour, from a single motif to multi-coloured patterning for knitters with a little experience.

We have designed eleven projects which are perfect for you, your home and to give as gifts to your loved ones. Each pattern is written in full hand, so you can really get to grips with focussing on the technique of intarsia knitting, and not have to worry about pattern abbreviations.

The technique section of the book is written in a way that we hope you will find clear and easy to follow.

One of the great things with intarsia knitting is you can try out your new techniques by just knitting a swatch and placing one of the charts from the book within your knitted piece. It's a really good way to experiment with colour, and not have the worry of working shaping or construction of a larger project design.

Start simple, with two contrasting colours, and make your way up to having designs with more colours and more intricate shapes.

Once you have mastered the projects in this book, you could always take one of our chart templates and add your own motif design. Just be sure to make your chart area exactly the same amount of stitches and rows, and you are good to go!

Quail Studio x

INTARSIA BASICS

Here we will show you the essential techniques for intarsia knitting: how to prepare your yarn and make yarn bobbins, how to calculate yarn quantities, how to join in and change colours and how to strand across the back for smaller areas.

what is intarsia knitting?

Intarsia is a colourwork technique that enables you to introduce colour into your knitting. It is used commonly to work blocks of colour or motifs which have a different colour to the background, with separate balls or bobbins of yarn in the new colour by your side as you work.

The key is to not carry the new yarn colour across the back of the work; it must be 'caught' by the working yarn. This will prevent holes in your work and keep the knitted fabric of a single thickness.

Intarsia cannot be worked in the round: as the yarn is in the wrong position, you would have to cut and reattach the yarn on each row and thus be left with multiple ends to weave in.

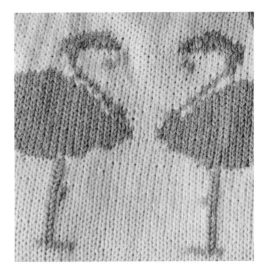

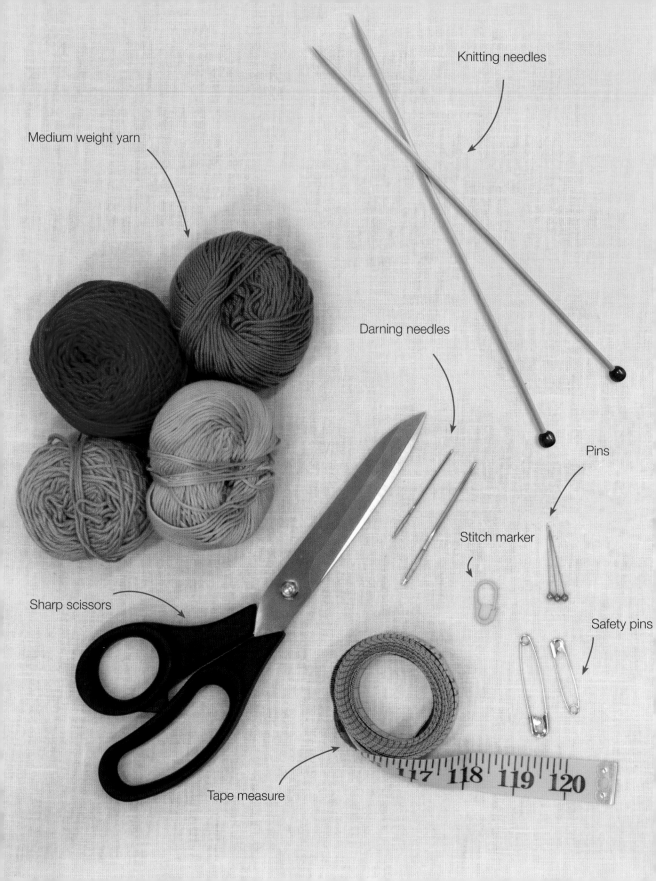

Knitting needles

Medium weight yarn

Darning needles

Pins

Stitch marker

Safety pins

Sharp scissors

Tape measure

117 118 119 120

useful materials

One of the great things about knitting is that you need very few things to get going – just knitting needles and some yarn and you are ready to go!

Like crochet hooks, knitting needles come in various sizes – all measured by the diameter of the needle. You will often find the size stamped on the top area of the needle. Knitting needles come in wood, plastic or metal and are also available in various different lengths.

The size of the needle, as well as the yarn you use with it, will determine the size of the stitches it produces. The most common needle sizes are 3.5–10mm (US 4–15), but finer needles are used for more intricate lace work.

OTHER EQUIPMENT:

I like to keep some items from my sewing basket handy, such as a pair of sharp scissors, a large darning needle, pins, safety pins and finally, a tape measure.

KNITTING NEEDLE SIZES AND CONVERSIONS

Metric	UK	US
2mm	14	0
2.25mm	13	1
2.5mm	12	-
2.75mm	12	2
3mm	11	3
3.25mm	10	3
3.5mm	9	4
3.75mm	9	5
4mm	8	6
4.5mm	7	7
5mm	6	8
5.5mm	5	9
6mm	4	10
6.5mm	3	10½
7mm	2	-
7.5mm	1	-
8mm	0	11
9mm	00	13
10mm	000	15
12mm		17
15mm		19
20mm		35
50mm		50

choosing yarn

It is important that you take plenty of time to choose the correct yarn and the best accompanying needles for your project. Yarns come in many different types and are available in a dazzling array of thicknesses, weights, colours and textures.

Usually the weight or type of yarn is printed on the label – also known as the ball band. The label will tell you the weight of the yarn, the gauge (or tension), the washing instructions, and the most suitable hook size to use.

If you are making a project that uses more than one ball of yarn, you will also need to check the 'dye lot' number on the ball band to ensure that the colour will be exactly the same. Some dye lots can vary so dramatically that when made up, your piece will look striped, as if you have used two different colour shades.

If you can't match the dye lots or are working with hand-dyed yarn, you can work alternate rows from two balls of yarn to avoid the stripy effect.

Yarn weight category	Super fine	Fine	Light	Medium	Bulky	Super bulky
	1	2	3	4	5	6
Type of yarns in category	4-ply, Sock	Sport	DK	Worsted	Chunky	Bulky
	Fingering	Baby	Light	Afghan, Aran	Craft, Rug	Roving
Knitting tension (gauge) ranges. Measured in stocking (stockinette) stitch over 10cm (4in)	27–32 sts	23–26 sts	21–24 sts	16–20 sts	12–15 sts	7–11 sts
Recommended needle in metric	2.25–3.25mm	3.25–3.75mm	3.75–4.5mm	4.5–5.5mm	5.5–8mm	8–12.75mm
Recommended needle in US size	1 to 3	3 to 5	5 to 7	7 to 9	9 to 11	11 to 17

abbreviations

Written patterns contain many abbreviations. These can differ depending upon whether you are following a US or UK pattern; always check the given abbreviations to make sure that you have understood the instructions. Because this book has been written to help you get started with understanding the stitches and without the need to worry about abbreviations, all of the patterns are written in long hand.

alt	alternate	P2tog	Purl 2 stitches together
beg	begin/beginning	patt	pattern
cont	continue	prev	previous
cm	centimetres	psso	pass slipped stitch over
dec	decrease(s)	rem	remain/remaining
DK	Double Knitting	rep	repeat
foll	follow/following	RS	Right side of work
g	grammes	S/M/L	Small/Medium/Large
g st	garter stitch	Sl 1	Slip 1 stitch
in	inch	st st	stocking (stockinette) stitch
inc	increase(s)	st(s)	stitch(es)
K	Knit	WS	Wrong side of work
K2tog	Knit 2 stitches together	yds	yards
m	metres	yfwd	yarn forward between needles
M1	Make 1 stitch	yb	yarn back between needles
meas	measures		
mm	millimetres		
P	Purl		

preparing yarn

Intarsia motifs often incorporate lots of different yarn colours but you will need only small amounts. If you decide to use whole balls when working these into your design, the yarns can get twisted and tangled – especially if the motif is more complex. To avoid this, you can use bobbins or make butterfly bobbins to keep your yarn organized and knot free when working with lots of separate colours.

You can purchase ready-made plastic bobbins to wrap your yarn around. These are quite small, so if you are using a bulkier yarn you may find not much yarn can be wound around them. A handmade bobbin made from a large piece of card, or tied in to a butterfly, is a useful, economical alternative.

Count how many separate bobbins your will need for your chart. The chart below would need six bobbins.

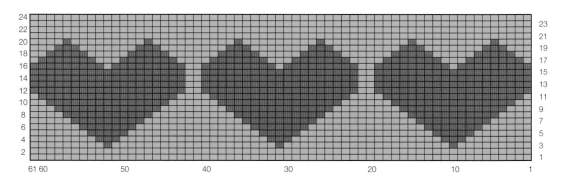

making a yarn butterfly

It can be helpful to practise making yarn butterflies with some left over yarn before using them in your work. This can also be a great way to store scraps of yarn.

1. Lay one end of yarn across your palm – this is the end that you will knit with.

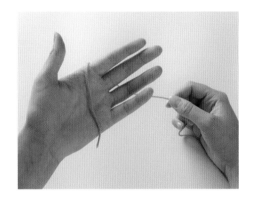

2. Take the other end of yarn around the back of your thumb, bring to the front and take around your second finger before going around your thumb again.

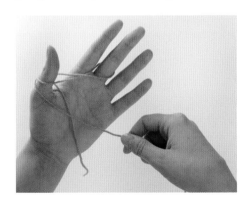

3. Keep winding the yarn like this until you are left with approx 15cm (6in) of yarn.

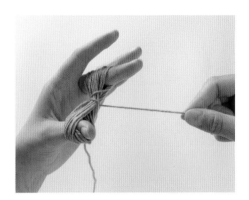

4. Wrap the remaining yarn around the centre of your bobbin. Tuck the end through one of these wraps to keep secure.

joining in a new colour

When working in intarsia you will find that you will have to change colour partway across the row, several times if you are working with multiple colours. You will need to follow the steps below for each new yarn or colour change.

1. On a knit row, work to the point you wish to change colour. Knit the next stitch with the new yarn.

2. Lay the new colour over the existing yarn with the tail to the left.

3. Bring the new colour under then over the existing colour.

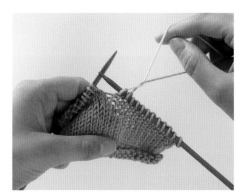

4. Knit the next stitch with the new colour. If you need to tighten the new colour, do so after you have knitted a few stitches. You only need to pull gently.

changing colour on a straight line

Once you have joined in your new colour, you may need to work a number of rows changing colour in the same place.

1. On a knit row, knit up to colour change. Bring the new colour up from under the old colour.

3. On a purl row, purl to the colour change. Bring the new colour from the left up under the old colour to the top.

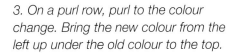

2. Drop the old colour so the new colour is ready to be worked.

4. Drop the old colour so the new colour is ready to be worked.

changing colour on a diagonal line

Often you will need to change colours diagonally. The technique for this is the same as for a straight line, but sometimes you will find that the yarn you need to use is in a different place. The technique for this is the same for both sides of work and for a right and left diagonal colour change.

1. On a knit row with a diagonal going to the right, bring the new colour up from underneath the old colour and knit.

3. On a purl row with the diagonal going to the right, bring the new colour up from underneath the old and purl.

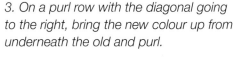

2. On a knit row with the diagonal going to the left, bring the new colour from underneath the old colour and knit.

4. On a purl row with the diagonal going to the left, bring the new colour up from underneath the old colour and purl.

stranding across a knit row

When working in intarsia you will sometimes need to carry the contrast colour across the back of the work for a few stitches in preparation for the next row. This is a technique also used in Fair Isle knitting.

1. Bring the contrast colour up from underneath the working yarn, knit the next stitch with the contrast yarn.

2. When stranding across the back you would normally do this every two to three stitches. When you are ready to catch the working yarn you wish to strand across the back, bring the contrast yarn up and over the working yarn from underneath and knit the next stitch.

3. The caught yarn will go under the next stitch. Knit the next stitch with the relevant yarn. Repeat steps 1 to 3.

stranding across a purl row

1. Bring the contrast colour up from underneath the background colour. Purl the next stitch with the contrast colour.

2. When stranding across the back you would normally do this every two to three stitches. When you are ready to catch the working yarn you wish to strand or carry across the back, bring the contrast yarn up and over the background yarn from underneath and purl the next stitch.

3. The caught yarn will go below the next stitch. Purl the next stitch with the relevant yarn. Repeat steps 1 to 3.

understanding tension (gauge)

Before you start on any knitting pattern, you need to understand the importance of tension. We have all been in the position where we are so eager to cast on with the beautiful yarn we have just purchased that we ignore the tension and hope for the best. But unfortunately that needs to change: it's time to get into tension!

THE TENSION (GAUGE) YOU ACHIEVE WHEN KNITTING

Most patterns will tell you the tension the designer has used in order to calculate the number of stitches and rows. For example: '20 sts and 28 rows to 10cm/4in measured over stocking stitch using 4mm needles'. You MUST knit a tension sample, before starting the oh-so-desirable project, to check that your tension matches that given.

Cast on at least four stitches more than the tension stated, so 24 stitches for the example above. This ensures the stitches you will measure will be whole stitches, and won't be sitting on the edge of the sample.

Work in the stitch pattern stated and for the number of rows stated, plus four rows more (so 32 rows in our example), for the same reasons as you cast on more stitches.

Cast off the sample and pin it out on an ironing board, without stretching the work.

Place a pin two stitches in from the right-hand side. Take a tape measure and measure 10cm/4in across from the pin, and place another pin. Now count the number of stitches between the two pins.

Then count the number of rows: place a pin, sideways, two rows down from the cast-off edge. Measure 10cm/4in down from the pin, and place another pin. Count the rows between the pins.

The numbers of stitches and rows are your natural tension with that yarn and those needles, over that stitch pattern. But this will change depending on the yarn and stitch pattern you are using. So with a pure wool DK you might be spot on to a given pattern tension, but when working with a cotton DK yarn, your knitting may be a bit looser. So you need to knit a tension sample EVERY TIME you embark on a new project.

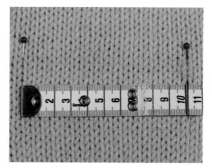

Measuring stitches in a tension square.

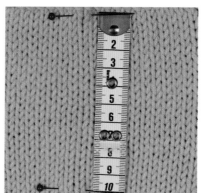

Measuring rows in a tension square.

working from charts

Colourwork patterns are usually shown on charts rather than written instructions. This makes the pattern easier to read and gives a visual guide as to what the motif will look like. Intarsia charts are mostly designed as motifs or pictures rather than repeats.

Each square of the chart represents one stitch and each line of the chart represents one row. The right side 'knit' or odd numbered rows are read from right to left. The wrong side 'purl' rows or even numbered rows are read from left to right, unless instructions say otherwise. Charts also start from the bottom up.

Different colours are shown either by colour or symbols. A key will show what each colour or symbol represents. Often a box with no colour or symbol will represent the main colour. Charts in grey indicate that the motif changes colour throughout

the design; a chart in colour shows that the motif appears in the colours shown throughout. Follow the written pattern instructions up to the point of placing your chart.

Your pattern will read similar to:
Next Row: Knit 4, work next 16 stitches as row 1 of chart, knit to end.

You will need to use a yarn bobbin or butterfly for the contrast colour and for the start of the row with the right side facing.

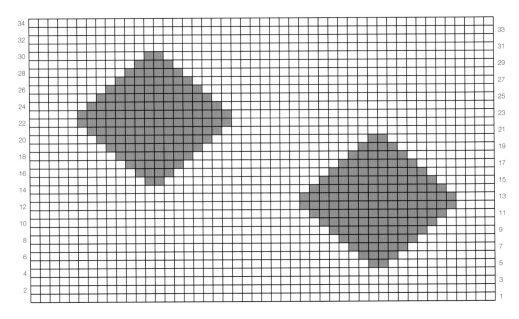

swiss darning

Depending on the design, you can work each colour as it appears on the chart, or you can work the large sections of colour and Swiss darn (known also as duplicate stitch) the small areas once knitting is complete. We suggest using this stitch if only a few stitches of an alternate colour are required.

1. Bring the point of the needle through from the back of the knitting, at the base of the stitch to be worked and pull through.

3. If you wish to work the row above, insert the point of the needle through the base of the last stitch from back to front.

2. Insert the needle behind the two loops of the stitch, from right to left, and pull through. Insert needle into same place where the stitching began and pull through from front to back.

4. Work as for steps 1 and 2 working from left to right.

finishing

When completing an intarsia project, you will be faced with many ends hanging from the wrong side of the work.

The first thing to do is to check the tension of the stitches around the joining areas. Using a tapestry needle, adjust the stitches to match in size by working in the direction of knitting.

When you are happy with the tension it is time to sew in the ends. You can use the tail end of the yarn to close the gaps; this will pull the stitches together.

To prevent the colours showing through on the right side of the work, keep the colours matching on the reverse.

When weaving in the ends, thread the tail ends of yarn through the purl 'bumps' on the wrong side of the work through the next few stitches, keeping to the edge of the motif if possible. It is always good to weave back down a few stitches to ensure it stays in place.

Pull the fabric a little before cutting off the excess.

When completing an intarsia project you should be able to tell the shape or design from the wrong side once the ends have been sewn in.

pressing and blocking

Having worked a section of intarsia, it is important to block it before finishing or sewing together, in order to make the work as smooth as possible.

Lay out the knitted piece without stretching it and pin it to a blocking board (or flat surface you don't mind pinning). It is very easy to over-stretch the fabric; if it's too stretched when you steam it, it can make the item too large. Ensure that the pieces are lying flat and are straight: for example, if blocking a sweater, the armholes should be at the same depth. It is always worth checking the measurements before you complete the pinning and begin the steaming process.

Now you can begin steaming. How you do this depends on the yarn you have pinned out. If it is pure cotton then you can have your iron on full steam and fairly hot.

For pure wool and wool-blend yarns, bring the steam setting down to a medium heat. If the yarn is particularly fine, then cover the pieces with a thin piece of linen fabric.

Simply hold the iron or steamer above the knitted pieces. (You may wish to place some weight on the fabric if you feel it needs extra pressure to smooth your intarsia.) Allow the knitting to dry and cool before removing the pins.

If the yarn is a heat sensitive fibre, such as 100% acrylic or mohair, then you need to cold-block it. Instead of using an iron or steamer, fill a clean water spray bottle – as used for indoor plants – and mist the pinned-out piece with water. Then cover it with a towel and pat dry. Allow to dry before removing the pins.

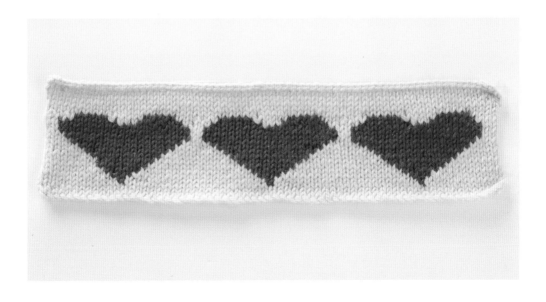

FOX PILLOW

PAGE 46

DRAUGHT
EXCLUDER
PAGE 50

TEA COSY

PAGE 54

DIAMOND PILLOW
PAGE 58

DOOR STOP

PAGE 62

CHEVRON SCARF

PAGE 66

CHILD'S HAT & MITTENS

PAGE 70

STAR BLANKET

PAGE 78

CHILD'S MOTIF
SWEATER

PAGE 82

FLAMINGO MOTIF
SWEATER

PAGE 90

PATTERNS

FOX
PILLOW

Instructions

SIZE
45 x 45cm (17¾ x 17¾in)

YARN
Rowan Pure Wool Superwash DK
or alternative DK (light worsted) yarn
made of 100% wool
A – Seville 113 x 5
B – Chalk 101 x 3

NEEDLES
4mm (UK 8 / US 6) needles

TENSION
22sts and 30 rows to 10cm/4in
Measured over stocking/stockinette stitch
using 4mm needles

EXTRAS
Black DK yarn to Swiss darn nose
and eyes
5 medium-size buttons
Pillow pad, 45 x 45cm (17¾ x 17¾in)

PILLOW
Using yarn A, cast on 99 stitches.
Row 1 (RS): Knit 1, * purl 1, knit 1; repeat
from * to end.
Repeat row 1 until work measures 30cm
(12in) from the cast-on edge, ending after a
wrong-side row.

PLACE CHART
Using the intarsia method shown on the
information pages (see pages 14–18 for
guidance), and working in stocking stitch,
start on a knit row and work rows 1–136 from
the chart (see page 48.)
Break off yarn B, and continue in yarn A only.

Next Row (RS): Knit 1, * purl 1, knit 1; repeat
from * to end.
Repeat last row until work measures 26cm
(10¼in) from last chart row, ending after a
wrong-side row.

Buttonhole Row (RS): Knit 1, (purl 1, knit 1) 3
times, * yarn forward, knit 2 together, (purl 1,
knit 1) 10 times; repeat from * 3 times more,
yarn forward, knit 2 together, purl 1, knit 1.
Next Row: Knit 1, * purl 1, knit 1; repeat from
* to end.
Repeat last row 3 times more.
Cast off in pattern.

MAKING UP
Press as described on the information page
(see page 23). Weave in all ends.

Using chart as a guide, Swiss darn nose and
eye details.
Folding buttonhole edge over back panel, join
side seams using mattress stitch.
Attach buttons.
Weave in remaining ends.
Insert pillow pad and fasten buttons.

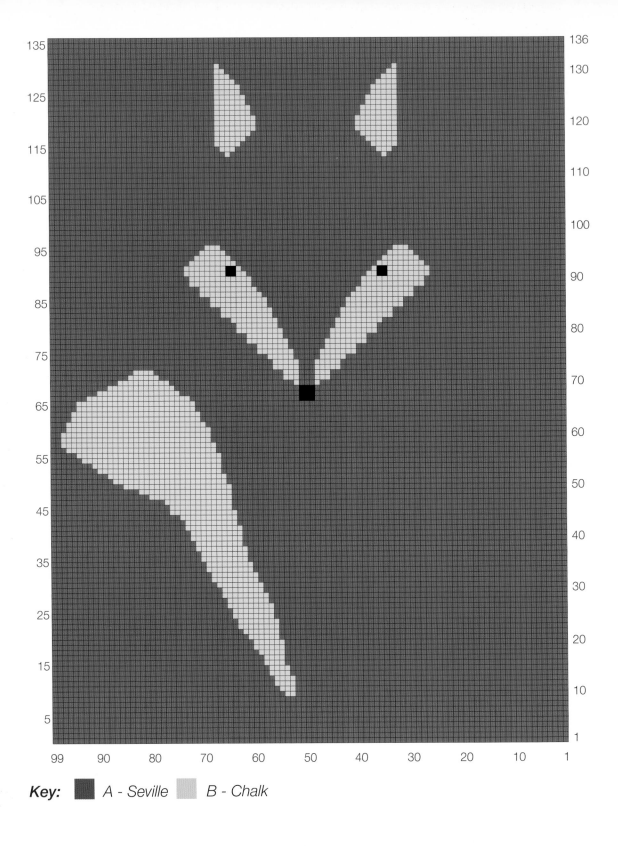

Key: A - Seville B - Chalk

DRAUGHT
EXCLUDER

Instructions

SIZE
11 x 97cm (4¼ x 38¼in)
(excluding pompoms)

YARN
Rowan Pure Wool Superwash worsted
or alternative aran (worsted) yarn made of
100% wool
A – Navy 149 x 3
B – Pretty Pink 113 x 1
C – Olive 125 x 1
D – Magenta 119 x 1
E – Periwinkle 146 x 1
F – Gold 133 x 1
G – Damson 150 x 1
H – Cardinal 136 x 1
I – Mallard 144 x 1

NEEDLES
4.5mm (UK 7 / US 7) needles

TENSION
16sts and 21 rows to 10cm/4in
Measured over stocking/stockinette stitch
using 4.5mm needles and yarn held
double throughout

EXTRAS
Pompom maker
Upholstery filling/batting, approx. 150g (5¼oz)

DRAUGHT EXCLUDER
Using yarn A held double, cast on 12 stitches.

PLACE CHART
Using the intarsia technique shown on the
information pages (see pages 14–18 for
guidance) and working in stocking stitch,
start with a knit row and work rows 1–23
from the desired chart (see pages 52 and 53.)
Cast off.

Sample shows:
Front – A, B, C, D, E, F, G, H, I, J, K, L, M
Worked in yarn A plus yarns B, C, D, E, F, G,
H, I, D, F, C, E and H.
Back – N, O, P, Q, R, S, T, U, V, W, X, Y, Z
Worked in yarn H, plus yarns F, A, D, F, A, E,
B, C, H, E, G and D.

Each panel has a total of 13 motifs.

MAKING UP
Press as described on the information page
(see page 23).

Join together 13 motifs for the front and 13
motifs for the back, using mattress stitch.
Join bottom seam and 2 side edges.
Using contrasting colours, make 6 pompoms
approx. 4cm (1½in) in diameter. Attach 3 to
each side seam.
Weave in all ends.

Seam along the top edge for a couple of
motifs, stuff, and seam a couple more.
Repeat until the draught excluder is full.
Weave in remaining ends.

Charts

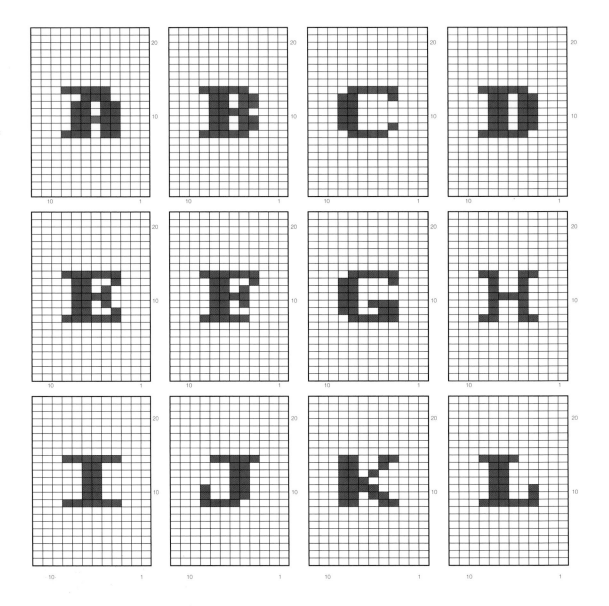

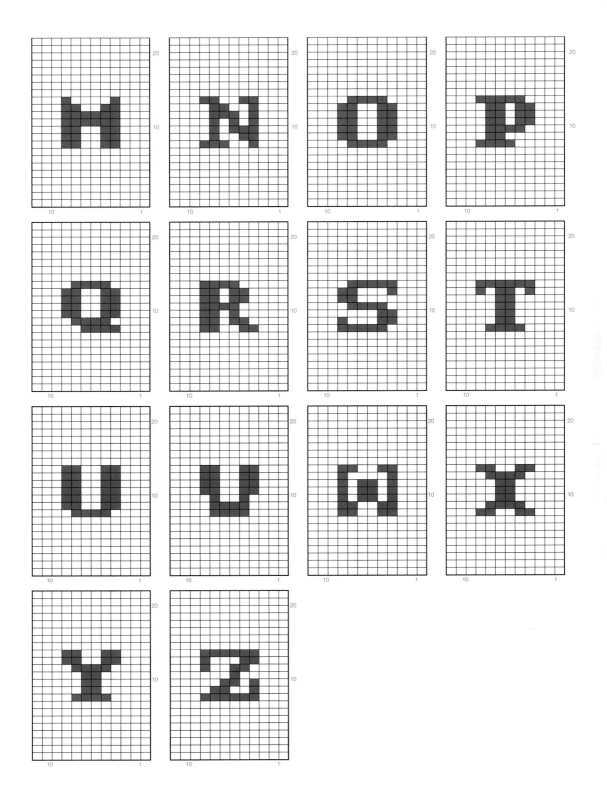

TEA
COSY

Instructions

SIZE

30 x 23cm (12 x 9in)
(this will fit a small/medium-size teapot)

YARN

Rowan Pure Wool Superwash worsted
or alternative aran (worsted) yarn made of
100% wool
A – Pretty Pink 113 x 1
B – Magenta 119 x 1

NEEDLES

4mm (UK 6 / US 8) needles
2 x 4mm (UK 8 / US 6) double-pointed
needles

TENSION

22sts and 28 rows to 10cm/4in
Measured over stocking/stockinette stitch
using 4mm needles

TEA COSY FRONT AND BACK – both alike

Using yarn A and 4mm needles, cast on
67 stitches.
Row 1 (RS): * Knit 1, purl 1; repeat from *
to last stitch, knit 1.
Repeat last row 5 times more.

Starting with a knit row, work 4 rows in
stocking stitch.

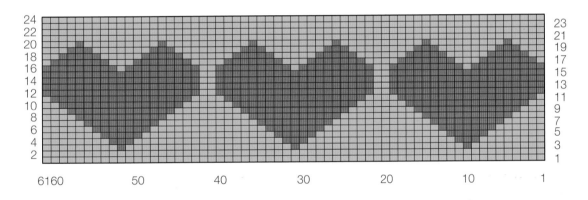

Key: ▨ A - Pretty Pink   ▨ B - Magenta

PLACE CHART

Using the intarsia technique shown on the information pages (see pages 14–18 for guidance), and working in stocking stitch, start with a knit row and place the chart as follows:

Next Row (RS): Using yarn A knit 3, work next 61 stitches as row 1 of the chart, using yarn A knit 3.

Next Row: Using yarn A purl 3, work next 61 stitches as row 2 of the chart, using yarn A purl 3.

These 2 rows set the stitches.

Continue as set until all 24 rows of the chart have been completed.

Break off yarn B, and continue in yarn A only. Starting with a knit row, work in stocking stitch until work measures 16cm (6¾in) from the cast-on edge, ending after a wrong-side row.

Next row (RS): Knit 2, slip 1, knit 1, pass slipped stitch over, knit to last 4 stitches, knit 2 together, knit 2. 65 stitches.

Next row: Purl 2, purl 2 together, purl to last 4 stitches, slip 1 purlwise, purl 1, pass slipped stitch over, purl 2. 63 stitches.

Repeat last 2 rows 11 times more.

19 stitches.

Cast off.

Work back as for front.

MAKING UP

Press as described on the information page (see page 23).

Join side seams together using mattress stitch.

Join top seam together using mattress stitch.

Using yarn B, make 3 pompoms approx. 6cm (2½in) in diameter. Attach to top seam. Weave in all ends.

DIAMOND
PILLOW

Instructions

SIZE
40 x 40cm (15¾ x 15¾in)

YARN
Rowan Baby Merino Silk DK or alternative DK
(light worsted) yarn made of blended wool
and silk

A – Iceberg 699 x 1
B – Deep 682 x 1
C – Emerald 685 x 1
D – Teal 677 x 1
E – Goldilocks 691 x 1
F – Leaf 692 x 1
G – Candy 695 x 1
H – Shell Pink 674 x 1
I – Dawn 672 x 1
J – Aubergine 701 x 1

NEEDLES
4mm (UK 8 / US 6) needles

TENSION
22sts and 30 rows to 10cm/4in
Measured over stocking/stockinette stitch
using 4mm needles

EXTRAS
Cushion pad, 40 x 40cm (15¾ x 15¾in)

PILLOW
Using yarn A, cast on 90 stitches.

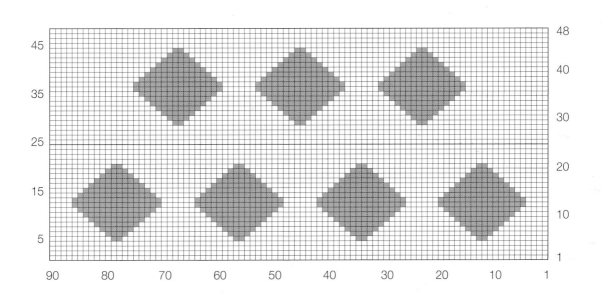

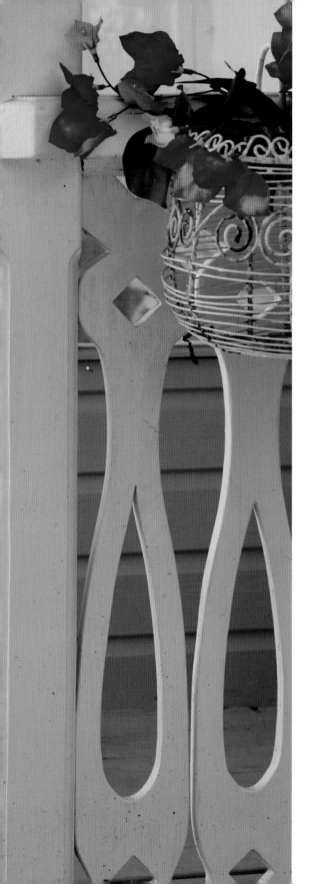

PLACE CHART

Using the intarsia technique shown on the information pages (see pages 14–18 for guidance), and working in stocking stitch, start with a knit row and work rows 1–48 from the chart 5 times, using the following colour sequence:

Rows 1–24: Background yarn A, Diamond yarn B.
Rows 25–48: Background C, Diamond D.
Rows 49–72: Background E, Diamond F.
Rows 73–96: Background G, Diamond H.
Rows 97–120: Background I, Diamond J.
Rows 121–144: Background B, Diamond A.
Rows 145–168: Background D, Diamond C.
Rows 169–192: Background F, Diamond E.
Rows 193–216: Background H, Diamond G.
Rows 217–240: Background J, Diamond I.

Cast off, using yarn J.

MAKING UP

Press as described on information page (see page 23).
Fold in half, and join both side seams using mattress stitch.
Weave in all ends.
Insert pillow pad and join top seam using mattress stitch.
Weave in remaining ends.

Instructions

SIZE
15 x 18cm (6 x 7in)
(excluding handle)

YARN
Rowan Pure Wool Superwash worsted
or alternative aran (worsted) yarn made of
100% wool
A – Oxford 148 x 1
B – Almond or Mole x 1
C – Pretty Pink 113 x 1
D – Magenta 119 x 1
E – Periwinkle 146 x 1

NEEDLES
4.5mm (UK 7 / US 7) needles

TENSION
20sts and 25 rows to 10cm/4in
Measured over stocking/stockinette
stitch using 4.5mm needles

EXTRAS
Sand or weights (approx. 600g / 21¼oz)
Upholstery filling (approx. 75g / 2¾oz)

FIRST PANEL (FRONT AND SIDES)
Using yarn A, cast on 92 stitches.
Row 1 (WS): Purl.

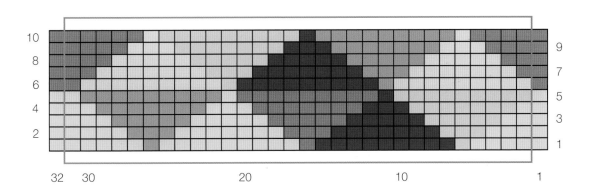

Key:
- A - Oxford
- B - Almond
- C - Pretty Pink
- D - Magenta
- E - Periwinkle

Using the intarsia technique shown on the information pages (see pages 14–18 for guidance), and working in stocking stitch, start with a knit row and work rows 1–10 from the chart 4 times, then rows 1–5 once more, repeating the 30 stitch pattern repeat 3 times across each row.

Next Row (WS): Using yarn A, purl to end.
Cast off.

SECOND PANEL (TOP, BACK AND BASE)

Using yarn A, cast on 32 stitches.
Row 1 (RS): Knit.
Continue to work in stocking stitch for 45 more rows, ending after a wrong-side row.

PLACE CHART

Using the intarsia technique, and working in stocking stitch, start with a knit row and work rows 1–10 from the chart 4 times, then rows 1–5 once more, repeating the 30-stitch pattern repeat once across each row.

Continuing in yarn A only, work a further 45 rows in stocking stitch, ending after a wrong-side row.
Cast off.

HANDLE

Using yarn D, cast on 32 stitches.
Starting with a knit row, work in stocking stitch until work measures 30cm (12in), ending after a wrong-side row.
Cast off.

MAKING UP

Press as described on the information page (see page 23).

Join the side edges of the first panel to the back section of the second panel (so chart pieces match) using mattress stitch.
Join the bottom edges of the first panel to the base section of the second panel using mattress stitch.
Weave in all ends.
Join two top edges of the first panel to the top section of the second panel, stuff, then join the remaining edge.

Handle

Press in half widthways and join seams using mattress stitch.
Using photo as a guide, attach handle to side edges of doorstop using slip stitch.
Weave in remaining ends.

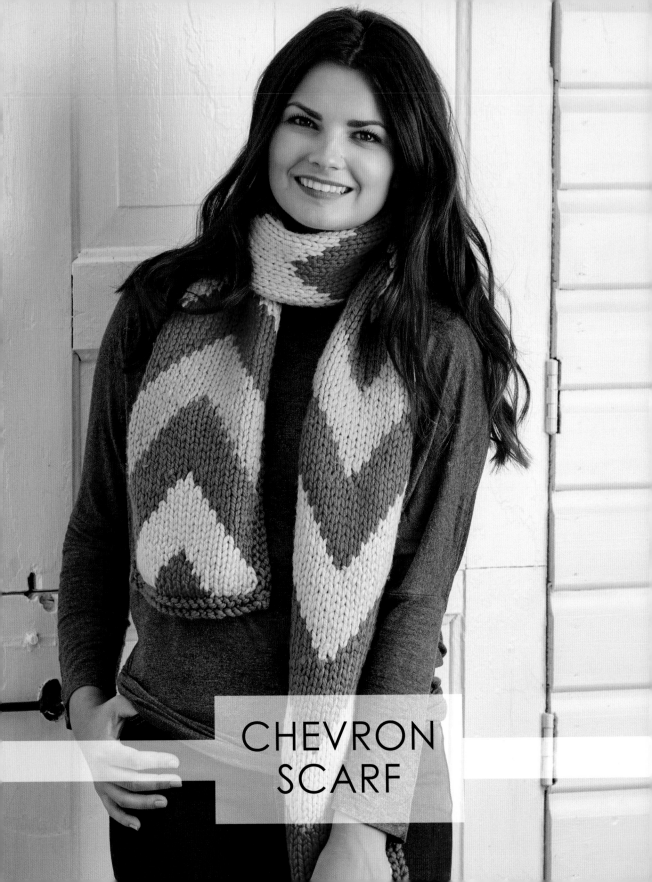

CHEVRON
SCARF

Instructions

SIZE

24 x 250cm (9½ x 98½in)

YARN

Rowan Big wool or alternative super chunky
(super bulky) 100% merino wool yarn
A – Glum 056 x 3
B – Linen 048 x 2
C – Pantomime 079 x 2
D – Yoke 078 x 2

NEEDLES

10mm (UK 000 / US 15) needles

TENSION

10sts and 10 rows to 10cm/4in
Measured over stocking/stockinette stitch
using 10mm needles

SCARF

Using yarn B cast on 20 stitches.

PLACE CHART

Using the intarsia technique shown on the
information pages (see pages 14–18 for
guidance), and working in stocking stitch,
start with a knit row and work rows
1–48 from the chart 4 times, then rows 1–56
once, repeating the 20-stitch pattern repeat
across each row (see page 48 for chart).

Cast off using yarn B.

MAKING UP

Press as described on the information page
(see page 23).

With right side facing and using yarn A, pick
up and knit 206 stitches up one side edge of
the scarf.

Starting with a knit row, work in garter stitch
for 2 rows.
Cast off.
Work other side of scarf to match.

With right side and using yarn A, pick up and
knit 24 stitches across cast-on edge and new
garter-stitch edges.
Starting with a knit row, work in garter stitch
for 2 rows.
Cast off.

Work cast-off edge to match.

Weave in all ends.

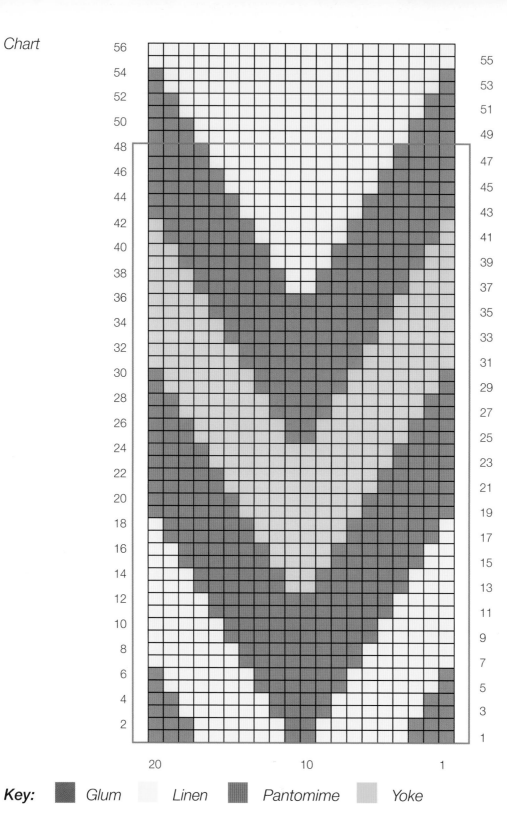

Key: ■ Glum □ Linen ■ Pantomime □ Yoke

CHILD'S
HAT

Instructions

SIZE

4–7(7–10) years
Finished circumference:
45(50)cm / 17¾(19¾)in

YARN

Rowan Softyak DK or alternative DK
(light worsted) yarn made of blended fibres,
including yak
A – Lea 236 x 1(1)
B – Terrain 243 x 1(1)
C – Plain 232 x 1(1)

NEEDLES

3.25mm (UK 10 / US 3) needles
4mm (UK 8 / US 6) needles

TENSION

22sts and 30 rows to 10cm/4in
Measured over stocking/stockinette
stitch using 4mm needles

EXTRAS

Pompom maker

HAT

Using yarn A and 3.25mm needles, cast on
98(110) stitches.
Row 1 (RS): Knit 2, * purl 2, knit 2; repeat
from * to end.
Row 2: Purl 2, * knit 2, purl 2; repeat from
* to end.
Repeat last 2 rows until work measures 4cm
(1½in) from the cast-on edge, ending after
a wrong-side row, increasing 1(2) stitches
evenly across the row. 99(112) stitches.

Break off yarn A.
Change to 4mm needles and yarn B.
Starting with a knit row, work in stocking
stitch for 6 rows.

Chart

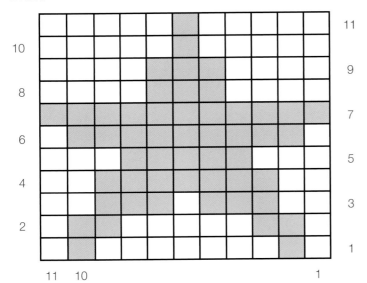

Key: ▪ Plain

Using the intarsia technique shown on the information pages (see pages 14–18 for guidance), and working in stocking stitch, start with a knit row and place the chart as follows:

Next row (RS): Knit 2, * work 11 stitches as row 1 of chart, knit 7; repeat from * to end.
Next row (WS): * Purl 7, work 11 stitches as row 2 of chart; repeat from * to last 2 stitches, purl 2.
These 2 rows set the stitches.
Continue as set until all 11 rows of chart have been completed, ending after a right-side row.

Break off yarn C, and continue in yarn B only. Starting with a purl row, work in stocking stitch until work measures 13(14)cm / 5¼(5½in) from the cast-on edge, ending after a wrong-side row.

Shape crown
Next Row (RS): * Knit 9(6), knit 2 together; repeat from * to end. 90(98) stitches.
Next Row: Purl.
Next Row: * Knit 7(5), knit 2 together; repeat from * to end. 80(84) stitches.
Next Row: Purl.
Next Row: * Knit 6(4), knit 2 together; repeat from * to end. 70(70) stitches.
Next Row: Purl.
Next Row: * Knit 5(3), knit 2 together; repeat from * to end. 60(56) stitches.
Next Row: Purl.
Next Row: * Knit 4(2), knit 2 together; repeat from * to end. 50(42) stitches.
Next Row: Purl. 2
Next Row: * Knit 3(2), knit 2 together; repeat from * to end. 40(28) stitches.
Next Row: Purl.
Next Row: * Knit 2(1), knit 2 together; repeat from * to end. 30(14) stitches.
Next Row: Purl.
Next Row: * Knit 1(0), knit 2 together; repeat from * to end. 20(7) stitches.

4–7 years only
Next Row (RS): K2tog to end. 10 stitches.
Next Row: Purl.

Cut yarn, leaving a tail long enough (approx. 30cm / 12in) to sew up hat.
Thread yarn through remaining stitches, but do not tighten.

MAKING UP
Press as described on the information page (see page 23).
Tighten the yarn tail threaded through remaining stitches, and join side seam using mattress stitch.
Using yarn C, make a pompom approx. 6cm (2½in) in diameter, and attach firmly to top of hat. Weave in all ends.

CHILD'S
MITTENS

Instructions

SIZE

4–7(7–10) years

Finished circumference: 15(21)cm / 6(8¼)in

Finished height: 16(20)cm / 6¼(7¾)in

YARN

Rowan Softyak DK or alternative DK
(light worsted) yarn made of blended fibres,
including yak

A – Lea 236 x 1(1)

B – Terrain 243 x 1(1)

C – Plain 232 x 1(1)

NEEDLES

3.25mm (UK 10 / US 3) needles

4mm (UK 8 / US 6) needles

2 x 3.25mm (UK 10 / US 3) double-pointed
needles

TENSION

22sts and 30 rows to 10cm/4in
Measured over stocking/stockinette stitch
using 4mm needles

MITTENS – make 2

Using yarn A and 3.25mm needles, cast on
34(46) stitches.

Row 1 (RS): Knit 2, * purl 2, knit 2; repeat
from * to end.

Row 2: Purl 2, * knit 2, purl 2; repeat from *
to end.

Repeat last 2 rows 6 times more.

Break off yarn A.

Change to 4mm needles and yarn B.
Starting with a knit row, work 6 rows in
stocking stitch.

PLACE CHART

Using the intarsia technique shown on the
information pages (see pages 14–18 for
guidance), and working in stocking stitch,
start with a knit row and place the chart (see
page 77) as follows:

Left mitten

Next Row (RS): Using yarn B knit 3(6), work
next 11 stitches as row 1 of chart, using yarn
B knit 20(29).

Next Row: Using yarn B purl 20(29), work
next 11 stitches as row 2 of chart, using yarn
B purl 3(6).

These 2 rows set the stitches.

Continue as set until all 11 rows of chart have
been completed.

Right mitten

Next Row (RS): Using yarn B knit 20(29),
work next 11 stitches as row 1 of chart, using
yarn B knit 3(6).

Next Row: Using yarn B purl 3(6), work next
11 stitches of row 2 of chart, using yarn B
purl 20(29).

These 2 rows set the stitches.

Continue as set until all 11 rows of chart have
been completed.

Break yarn C, and continue in yarn B only.
Starting with a purl row, work 11(17) rows in
stocking stitch.

Mitten top

Next Row (RS): * Knit 1, knit 2 together, knit
11(17), slip 1, knit 1, pass slipped stitch over,
knit 1; repeat from * once more.

30(42) stitches.

Next Row: Purl.
Next Row: * Knit 1, knit 2 together, knit 9(15), slip 1, knit 1, pass slipped stitch over, knit 1; repeat from * once more. 26(38) stitches.
Next Row: Purl.
Next Row: * Knit 1, knit 2 together, knit 7(13), slip 1, knit 1, pass slipped stitch over, knit 1; repeat from * once more. 22(34) stitches.
Next Row: Purl.
Next Row: * Knit 1, knit 2 together, knit 5(11), slip 1, knit 1, pass slipped stitch over, knit 1; repeat from * once more. 18(30) stitches.
Next Row: Purl.
Next Row: * Knit 1, knit 2 together, knit 3(9), slip 1, knit 1, pass slipped stitch over, knit 1; repeat from * once more. 14(26) stitches.
Next Row: Purl.
Next Row: * Knit 1, knit 2 together, knit 1(7), slip 1, knit 1, pass slipped stitch over, knit 1; repeat from * once more. 10(22) stitches.
Next Row: Purl.

4 – 7 years only

Next Row (RS): Knit 5, and break yarn, leaving a tail long enough to sew up the mitten (approx. 30cm / 12in).

7 – 10 years only

Next Row (RS): * Knit 1, knit 2 together, knit 5, slip 1, knit 1, pass slipped stitch over, knit 1; repeat from * once more. 18 stitches.
Next Row: Purl.
Next Row: * Knit 1, knit 2 together, knit 3, slip 1, knit 1, pass slipped stitch over, knit 1; repeat from * once more. 14 stitches.
Next Row: Purl.
Next Row: * Knit 1, knit 2 together, knit 1, slip 1, knit 1, pass slipped stitch over, knit 1; repeat from * once more. 10 stitches.
Next Row: Purl.
Next Row: Knit 5, and break yarn, leaving a tail long enough to sew up the mitten (approx. 30cm / 12in).

MAKING UP

Press as described on information page (see page 23).

Graft mitten top

Hold needles together with wrong sides facing.
On the front needle, go through the first stitch as if to purl; do not drop the stitch off the needle.
On the back needle, go through the first stitch as if to knit: do not drop the stitch off the needle.
Step 1: On the front needle, go through the first stitch as if to knit: drop the stitch off the needle.
Step 2: On the front needle, go through the new first stitch as if to purl: do not drop the stitch off the needle.
Step 3: On the back needle, go through the first stitch as if to purl; drop the stitch off the needle.
Step 4: On the back needle, go through the new first stitch as if to knit; do not drop the stitch off the needle.
Repeat the last 4 steps until all stitches are worked.

Join side seam using mattress stitch.

I-cord

Using yarn A and 3.25mm double-pointed needles, cast on 3 stitches.
Knit these 3 stitches, * slide these stitches to other end of needle, do not turn, pull the yarn across the back of the knitted stitches and knit into the right-most stitch, knit remaining stitches, repeat from * until i-cord measures 70cm (27½in).
Cast off.

Join a mitten to each end of the i-cord on the join seam.
Weave in all ends.

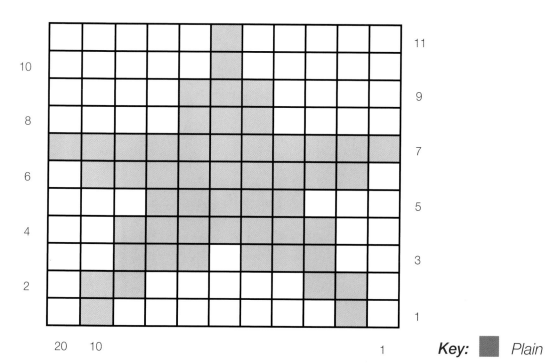

11

10

9

8

7

6

5

4

3

2

1

20   10   1

Key: ■ *Plain*

STAR
BLANKET

Instructions

SIZE

70 x 65cm (27½ x 25½in)

YARN

Rowan Baby Merino Silk DK or alternative DK
(light worsted) yarn made of blended wool
and silk
A – Straw 671 x 4
B – Bluebird 684 x 1
C – Shell Pink 674 x 1
D – Iceberg 699 x 1
E – Emerald 685 x 1
F – Goldilocks 691 x 1
G – Dawn 672 x 1
H – Cloud 693 x 1
I – Candy 695 x 1
J – Leaf 692 x 1
K – Aubergine 701 x 1

NEEDLES

4mm (UK 8 / US 6) needles

TENSION

22sts and 30 rows to 10cm/4in
Measured over stocking/stockinette stitch
using 4mm needles

BLANKET

Using yarn A and 4mm needles, cast on 154
stitches.
Row 1 (RS): * Purl 1, knit 1; repeat from * to end.
Row 2: * Knit 1, purl 1; repeat from * to end.
Repeat last 2 rows 8 times more.

Next Row (RS): Purl 1, * knit 1, purl 1; repeat
from * 6 times more, knit to last 15 stitches,
purl 1, * knit 1, purl 1; repeat from * 6 times
more.

Next Row: Purl 1, * knit 1, purl 1; repeat from
* 6 times more, purl to last 15 stitches, purl 1,
* knit 1, purl 1; repeat from * 6 times more.
Repeat last 2 rows 2 times more.

PLACE CHART

Using the intarsia technique shown on the
information pages (see pages 14–18 for
guidance), and working in stocking stitch,
starting with a knit row, use the photo as a
guide for colour placement and place the
chart (see page 80) as follows:
Next Row (RS): Purl 1, * knit 1, purl 1; repeat
from * 6 times more, ** knit 13, work next 24
stitches as row 1 from chart, repeat from **
2 times more, knit 13, purl 1, * knit 1, purl 1;
repeat from * 6 times more.
Next Row: Purl 1, * knit 1, purl 1; repeat
from * 6 times more, ** purl 13, work next 24
stitches as row 2 from chart, repeat from **
2 times more, purl 13, * purl 1, knit 1; repeat
from * 6 times more, purl 1.
These two rows set the stitches.
Continue as set until all 22 rows of the chart
have been completed.

Last 28 rows (chart plus 6 preceding rows) set pattern.
Keeping above correct, repeat last 28 rows, using the photo as a guide for colour placement, 5 times more.

Next Row (RS): Purl 1, * knit 1, purl 1; repeat from * 6 times more, knit to last 15 stitches, * purl 1, knit 1; repeat from * 6 times more, purl 1.
Next Row: Purl 1, * knit 1, purl 1; repeat from * 6 times more, purl to last 15 stitches, * purl 1, knit 1; repeat from * 6 times more, purl 1.
Repeat last 2 rows 2 times more.

Row 1 (RS): * Purl 1, knit 1; repeat from * to end.
Row 2: *Knit 1, purl 1; repeat from * to end.
Repeat last 2 rows 8 times more.
Cast off.

MAKING UP
Press as described on the information page (see page 23).
Weave in all ends.

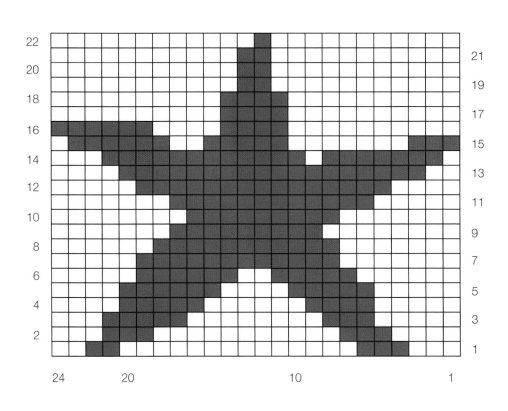

CHILD'S MOTIF
SWEATER

Instructions

SIZE
2–3(4–5, 6–7, 8–9) years

Finished size
35.5(37, 39, 41)cm
14(14½,15¼,16¼)in

YARN
Rowan Summerlite DK or alternative DK (light worsted) yarn made of 100% cotton
A – Favourite Denim 469 x 1
B – Silvery Blue 468 x 5(5,6,6)
C – Summer 453 x 1
D – Coral Blush 467 x 1
E – Cantaloupe 456 x 1
F – Sailor Blue 470 x 1
G – White 465 x 1

NEEDLES
3mm (UK 12 / US 2 or 3) needles
3.75mm (UK 9 / US 5) needles

TENSION
22sts and 30 rows to 10cm/4in
Measured over stocking/stockinette stitch using 3.75mm needles

EXTRAS
Stitch holders

BACK
Using yarn A and 3mm needles, cast on 78(82,86,90) stitches.
Row 1 (RS): Knit 2, * purl 2, knit 2; repeat from * to end.
Row 2: * Purl 2, knit 2; repeat from * to last 2 stitches, purl 2.
Repeat last 2 rows 4 times more, increasing 1 stitch at each end of last row. 80(84,88,92) stitches.
Break off yarn A.

Change to 3.75mm needles and yarn B. Starting with a knit row, work in stocking stitch until work measures 26(28,30,34)cm / 10¼(11,11¾,13½)in from the cast-on edge, ending after a wrong-side row.

SHAPE ARMHOLES
Cast off 3 stitches at beginning of next 2 rows. 74(78,82,86) stitches.
Next Row (RS): Knit 2, slip 1, knit 1, pass slipped stitch over, knit to last 4 stitches, knit 2 together, knit 2. 72(76,80,84) stitches.
Next Row: Purl.
Repeat last 2 rows 2 times more. 68(72,76,80) stitches.

Continue straight in stocking stitch until armhole measures 14(14,15,15)cm / 5½(5½,6,6)in, ending after a wrong-side row.

SHAPE BACK NECK AND SHOULDERS
Next Row (RS): Knit 18(19,20,21) stitches, and turn, leaving remaining stitches on a stitch holder.
Next Row: Purl 2, purl 2 together, purl to end. 17(18,19,20) stitches.
Cast off.

With right side facing, slip next 32(34,36,38) stitches onto another stitch holder, knit to end. 18(19,20,21) stitches.
Complete to match right shoulder, reversing shapings.

FRONT
Using yarn A and 3mm needles, cast on 78(82,86,90) stitches.
Row 1 (RS): Knit 2, * purl 2, knit 2, repeat from * to end.
Row 2: * Purl 2, knit 2, repeat from * to last 2 stitches, purl 2.

Repeat last 2 rows 4 times more, increasing 1 stitch at each end of last row. 80(84,88,92) stitches.
Break off yarn A.

Change to 3.75mm needles and yarn B. Starting with a knit row, work in stocking stitch for 30(34,38,44) rows.

PLACE CHART AND SHAPE ARMHOLES

Using the intarsia technique shown on the information pages (see pages 14 –18 for guidance), and working in stocking stitch, start with a knit row and place chart as follows:
Next Row (RS): Using yarn B knit 20(22,24,26) stitches, work next 40 stitches as row 1 of the chart.
Next Row: Using yarn B purl 20(22,24,26), work next 40 stitches as row 2 of chart.
These 2 rows set the stitches.
Continue as set until all 60 rows of the chart have been completed AND AT THE SAME TIME when work measures 26(28,30,34)cm / 10¼(11,12,13⅜)in from the cast-on edge, ending after a wrong-side row, cast off 3 sts at beginning of next 2 rows.
74(78,82,86) stitches.
Next Row (RS): Knit 2, slip 1, knit 1, pass slipped stitch over, knit to last 4 stitches, knit 2 together, knit 2. 72(76,80,84) stitches.
Next Row: Purl.
Repeat last 2 rows 2 times more.
68(72,76,80) stitches.

Once chart has been completed, continue straight in stocking stitch in yarn B only until 15 rows less have been worked than on back to start of shoulder shaping, ending after a wrong-side row.

SHAPE FRONT NECK AND SHOULDERS

Next Row (RS): Knit 25(27,29,31), and turn, leaving remaining stitches on a stitch holder.
Next Row: Purl.
Next Row: Knit to last 4 stitches, knit 2

together, knit 2. 24(26,28,30) stitches.
Next Row: Purl 2, slip 1 purlwise, purl 1, pass slipped stitch over, purl to end.
23(25,27,29) stitches.
Repeat last 2 rows until 17(18,19,20) stitches remain.
Continue straight for 6(5,4,3) rows.
Cast off.

With right side facing, slip next 18 stitches onto another holder, knit to end.
Complete to match left shoulder, reversing shapings.

SLEEVES

Using yarn A and 3mm needles, cast on 30(30,34,34) stitches.
Row 1 (RS): Knit 2, * purl 2, knit 2; repeat from * to end.
Row 2: * Purl 2, knit 2; repeat from * to last 2 stitches, purl 2.
Repeat last 2 rows 4 times more.
Break off yarn A.

Change to 3.75mm needles and yarn B.
Next Row: Knit 2, make 1, knit to last 2 stitches, make 1, knit 2.
32(32,36,36) stitches.
Working sleeve increases as set, increase 1 stitch as each end of every following 4th(4th,4th,6th) row to 60(60,66,66) stitches.
Continue straight in stocking stitch until work measures 26(30,34,38)cm / 10¼(11¾,13½,15)in from the cast-on edge, ending after a wrong-side row.

Cast off 3 stitches at beginning of next 2 rows. 54(54,60,60) stitches.
Next Row (RS): Knit 2, slip 1, knit 1, pass slipped stitch over, knit to last 4 stitches, knit 2 together, knit 2. 52(52,58,58) stitches.
Next Row: Purl.
Rep last 2 rows 2 times more.
48(48,54,54) stitches.
Work 1 row.
Cast off.

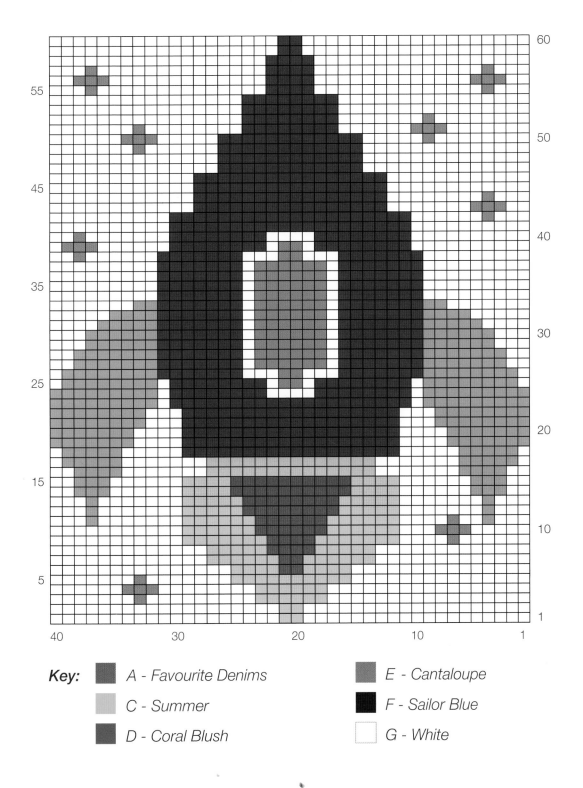

Key:

■	A - Favourite Denims	■	E - Cantaloupe
■	C - Summer	■	F - Sailor Blue
■	D - Coral Blush	□	G - White

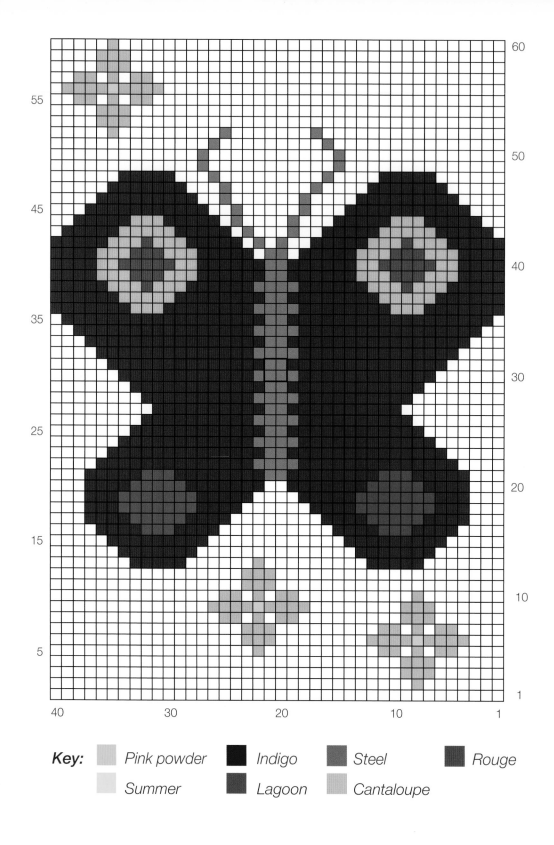

Key:

	Pink powder		Indigo		Steel		Rouge
	Summer		Lagoon		Cantaloupe		

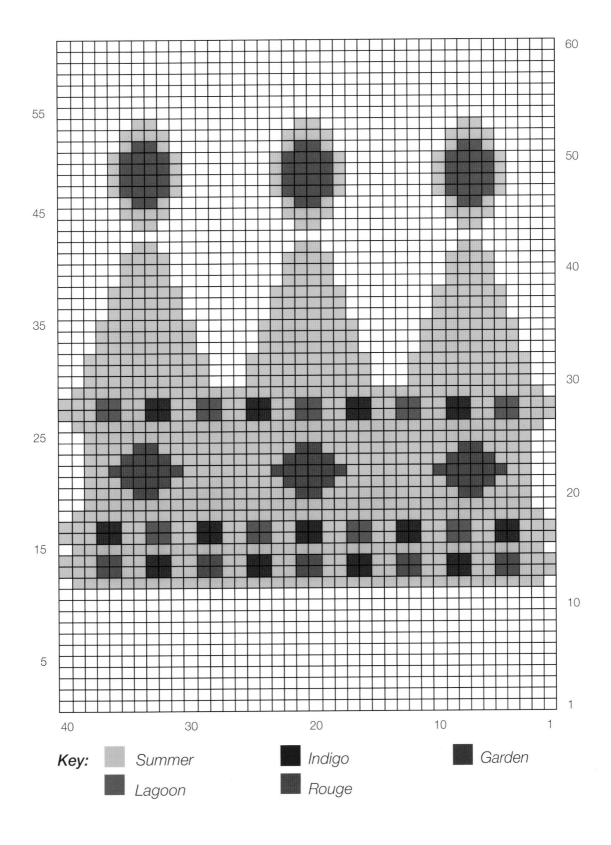

Key: Summer Indigo Garden
Lagoon Rouge

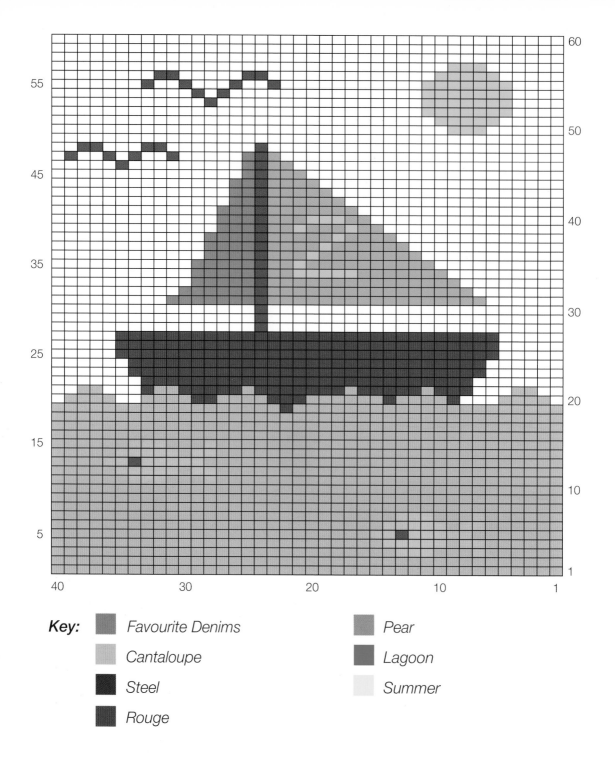

Key:

■ Favourite Denims	■ Pear
■ Cantaloupe	■ Lagoon
■ Steel	■ Summer
■ Rouge	

MAKING UP

Press as described on the information page (see page 23).

Join right shoulder seam using mattress stitch or back stitch if preferred.

NECKBAND

With right side facing, using yarn A and 3mm needles, pick up and knit 14 stitches down left front neck, knit 18 stitches from front neck stitch holder, pick up and knit 14 stiches up right front neck, knit 32(34,36,38) stitches from back neck stitch holder, decreasing 0(2,0,2) stitches in the middle of the back neck stitches. 78(78,82,82) stitches.

Row 1 (RS): Knit 2, * purl 2, knit 2; repeat from * to end.

Row 2: * Purl 2, knit 2; repeat from * to last 2 stitches, purl 2.

Repeat last 2 rows 2 times more.

Cast off, using 3.75mm needles.

Join left shoulder and neckband seam.
Join side and sleeve seams using mattress stitch.
Weave in all ends.

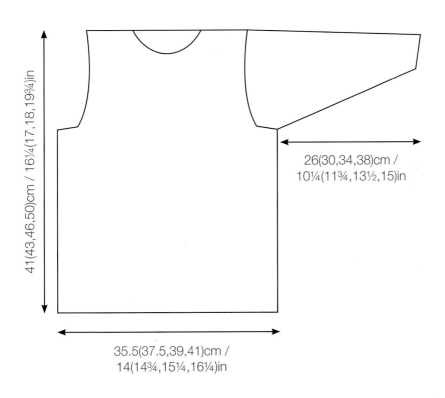

41(43,46,50)cm / 16¼(17,18,19¾)in

26(30,34,38)cm /
10¼(11¾,13½,15)in

35.5(37.5,39,41)cm /
14(14¾,15¼,16¼)in

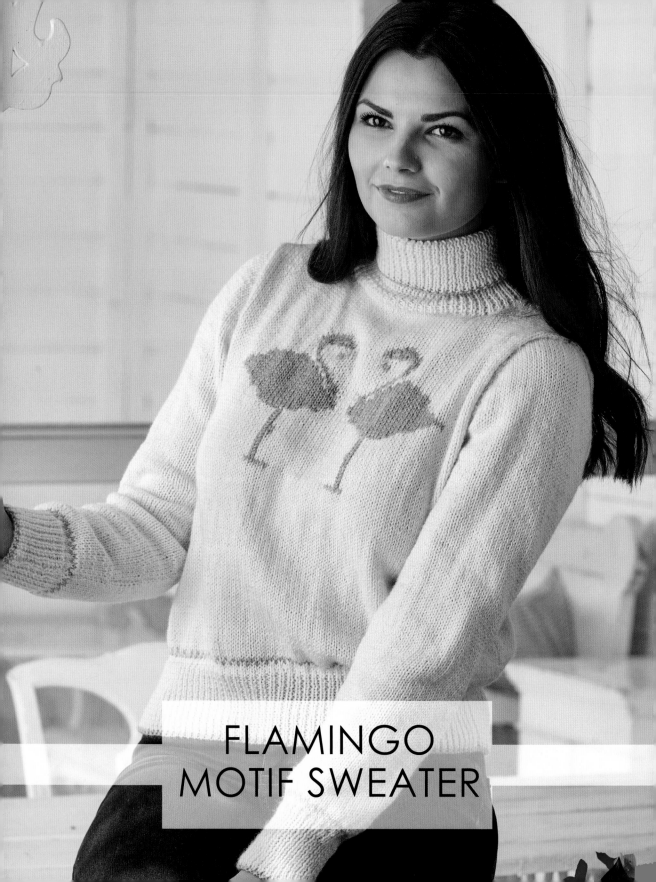

FLAMINGO
MOTIF SWEATER

Instructions

SIZE
S(M,L,XL)

To fit chest:
81–86(91–97,102–107,112–117)cm /
32–34(36–38,40–42,44–46)in

Finished size:
99(106,112,117)cm / 39(41¾,44,46)in

YARN
Rowan Baby Merino Silk DK (or alternative DK (light worsted) yarn made of blended wool and silk)
A – Snowdrop 670 x 9(9,10,11)
B – Candy 695 x 1(1,1,1)
C – Goldilocks 691 x 1(1,1,1)
D – Dawn 672 x 1(1,1,1)

NEEDLES
3.25mm (UK 10 / US 3) needles
4mm (UK 8 / US 6) needles

TENSION
22sts and 30 rows to 10cm/4in
Measured over stocking/stockinette stitch using 4mm needles

EXTRAS
Stitch holders

BACK
Using 3.25mm needles and yarn B, cast on 111(123,133,145) stitches.
Break off yarn B. Join in yarn A.
Row 1 (RS): *Knit 1, purl 1; repeat from * to last stitch, knit 1.
Row 2: Purl 1, * knit 1, purl 1; repeat from * to end.
Repeat last 2 rows until work measures 8cm (3⅛in) from the cast-on edge, ending after a wrong-side row.
Change to 4mm needles.
Starting with a knit row, work in stocking stitch for 2 rows.
Next Row (RS): * Using yarn A knit 1, using yarn B knit 1; repeat from * to last stitch, using yarn A knit 1.
Next Row: * Using yarn B purl 1, using yarn A purl 1; repeat from * to last stitch, using yarn B purl 1.

Break off yarn B, and continue in yarn A only.
Starting with a knit row, work in stocking stitch until work measures 34(35,35,35)cm / 13¼(13¾,13¾,13¾)in from the cast-on edge, ending after a wrong-side row.

SHAPE ARMHOLES
Cast off 5(6,6,7) stitches at beginning of next 2 rows. 101(111,121,131) stitches.
Decrease 1 stitch at each end of next 7(7,9,9) rows then on following 2(3,3,4) alternate rows, then on following 4th row. 81(89,95,103) stitches.

Continue straight in stocking stitch until armhole measures 20(20,21,22)cm/ 8(8,8¼,8¾)in, ending after a wrong-side row.

SHAPE BACK NECK AND SHOULDERS
Cast off 6 stitches at beginning of next 2 rows. 69(77,83,91) stitches.
Next Row (RS): Cast off 6 stitches, knit until there are 9(13,15,19) stitches on right-hand needle, and turn, leaving remaining stitches on a stitch holder.
Cast off 4(6,7,9) stitches at beginning of next row. 5(7,8,10) stitches.
Cast off.

With right side facing, slip next 39(39,41,41) stitches onto another stitch holder, knit to end. 15(19,21,25) stitches.
Complete to match right shoulder, reversing shapings.

FRONT

Using 3.25mm needles and yarn B, cast on 111(123,133,145) stitches.
Break off yarn B. Join in yarn A.
Row 1 (RS): *Knit 1, purl 1; repeat from * to last stitch, knit 1.
Row 2: Purl 1, * knit 1, purl 1; repeat from * to end.
Repeat last 2 rows until work measures 8cm (3⅛in) from the cast-on edge, ending after a wrong side row.

Change to 4mm needles.
Starting with a knit row, work in stocking stitch for 2 rows.
Next Row (RS): * Using yarn A knit 1, using yarn B knit 1; repeat from * to last stitch, using yarn A knit 1.
Next Row: * Using yarn B purl 1, using yarn A purl 1; repeat from * to last stitch, using yarn B purl 1.

Break off yarn B, and continue in yarn A only.
Starting with a knit row, work in stocking stitch until work measures 28(29,29,29)cm / 11(11½,11½,11½)in from the cast-on edge, ending after a wrong-side row.

PLACE CHART AND SHAPE ARMHOLES

Next Row (RS): Using yarn A knit 26(32,37,43) stitches, work next 59 stitches as row 1 of the chart, using yarn A knit 26(32,37,43) stitches.
Next Row: Using yarn A purl 26(32,37,43), work next 59 stitches as row 2 of the chart, using yarn A purl 26(32,37,43) stitches.
These 2 rows set the stitches.
Continue as set until all 47 rows of the chart have been completed AND AT SAME TIME when work measures 34(35,35,35)cm /

13¼(13¾,13¾,13¾)in from the cast-on edge, ending after a wrong-side row, cast off 5(6,6,7) stitches at beginning of next 2 rows. 101(111,121,131) stitches.
Decrease 1 stitch at each end of next 7(7,9,9) rows then on following 2(3,3,4) alternate rows, then on following 4th row. 81(89,95,103) stitches.

Continue straight in stocking stitch in yarn A only until 10(10,12,12) rows less have been worked than on back to start of shoulder shaping, ending after a wrong-side row.

SHAPE FRONT NECK AND SHOULDERS

Next row (RS): Knit 26(30,33,37), and turn, leaving remaining stitches on a stitch holder.

Decrease 1 stitch at neck edge of next 4 rows, then on following 1(1,2,2) alternate row(s). 21(25,27,31) stitches.
Work 1 row, ending after a wrong-side row.
Cast off 6 stitches at beginning of next and following alternate row. 9(13,15,19) stitches.
Work 1 row.
Cast off 4(6,7,9) stitches at beginning of next row. 5(7,8,10) stitches.
Work 1 row.
Cast off remaining stitches.

With right side facing, slip next 29 stitches onto another stitch holder, knit to end. 26(30,33,37) stitches.
Complete to match left shoulder, reversing shapings.

SLEEVES

Using 3.25mm needles and yarn B, cast on 58(60,62,64) stitches.
Break off yarn B. Join in yarn A.
Row 1 (RS): *Knit 1, purl 1; repeat from * to end.
Repeat last row until work measures 8cm (3⅛in) from cast-on edge, ending after a wrong-side row.

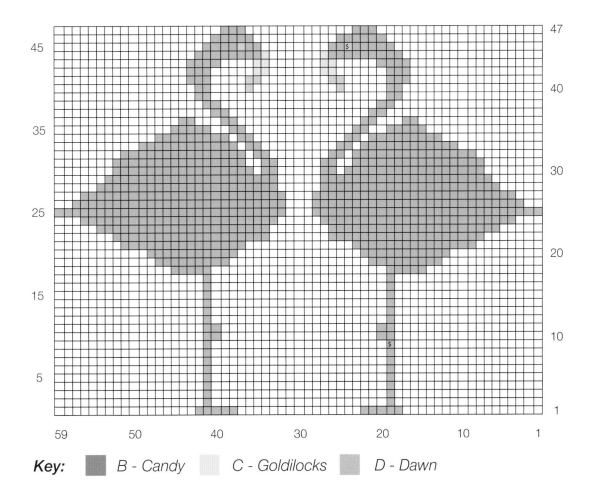

Key: B - Candy   C - Goldilocks   D - Dawn

Change to 4mm needles.
Starting with a knit row, work in stocking stitch for 2 rows.
Next row (RS): * Using yarn A knit 1, using yarn B knit 1; repeat from * to end.
Next row: * Using yarn A purl 1, using yarn B purl 1; repeat from * to end.

Break off yarn B, and continue in yarn A only.
Next Row (RS): Knit 2, make 1, knit to last 2 stitches, make 1, knit 2.
60(62,64,66) stitches.
Working all sleeve increases as set in last row, increase 1 stitch at each end of the 14th (14th,14th,12th) row and every following 10th row to 78(80,84,88) stitches.

Continue straight in stocking stitch until sleeve measures 46(47,48,49)cm / 18⅛(18½,19,19¼)in from the cast-on edge, ending after a wrong-side row.

SHAPE SLEEVE TOP
Cast off 5(5,5,3) stitches at beginning of next 2 rows. 64(64,66,68) stitches.
Decrease 1 stitch at each end of next 3 rows, then on following alternate row, then on the 6 following 4th rows. 44(44,46,48) stitches.
Work 1 row.
Decrease 1 stitch at each end of next row and every following alternate row to 38 stitches, then on every following row to 24 stitches.
Cast off.

MAKING UP

Press as described on the information page (see page 23).
Join right shoulder seam using mattress stitch.

COLLAR

With right side facing, using 3.25mm needles and yarn A, pick up and knit 12(12,14,14) stitches down left side of neck, knit 35 stitches from front neck holder, pick up and knit 12(12,14,14) stitches up right side of neck, then pick up and knit 39(39,41,41) stitches from back neck holder. 98(98,104,104) stitches.

Next Row (RS): *Knit 1, purl 1; repeat from * to end.
Repeat last row until work measures 15cm (6in) from the picked-up edge, ending after a wrong-side row.

Break off yarn A. Join in yarn B.
Cast off.

Join left shoulder and neckband seam.
Sew in sleeves.
Join side and sleeve seams.
Weave in all ends.

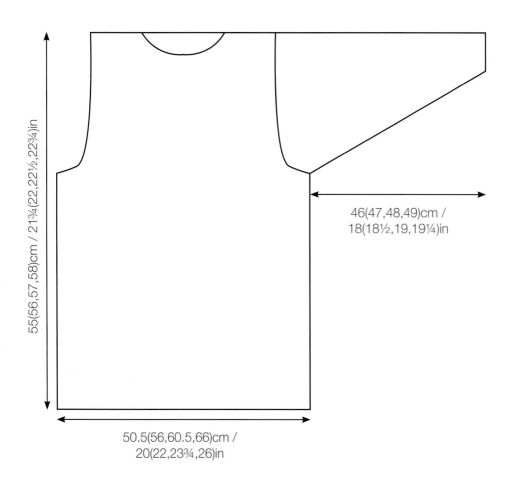

55(56,57,58)cm / 21¾(22,22½,22¾)in

46(47,48,49)cm /
18(18½,19,19¼)in

50.5(56,60.5,66)cm /
20(22,23¾,26)in

We would like to thank everybody who has helped bring this book together.

Special thanks also to Rowan for supporting the book with yarn sponsorship.

Finally, we would like to thank the team at Search Press for making this book possible.

Quail Studio

Published in 2019 by
Search Press Ltd
Wellwood, North Farm Road
Tunbridge Wells
Kent, TN2 3DR
United Kingdom

ISBN: 978-1-78221-318-5

Conceived, designed and produced by
Quail Publishing
The Old Town Hall,
Market Square,
Buckingham,
MK18 1NJ

Art Editor: Georgina Brant
Designers: Quail Studio
Photography: Jesse Wild
Creative Director: Darren Brant
Yarn Support: Rowan Yarns

Suppliers
If you have difficulty in obtaining any of the materials and equipment mentioned in this book, please visit the Search Press website for details of suppliers: www.searchpress.com